IMAGES
of America

SOMERVILLE

MAIN STREET, 1822. This pen-and-ink sketch of Main Street originally appeared in one of Somerville's early newspapers. Main Street literally was Somerville in those early days. (SCHS.)

Somerville Historic Advisory Committee

First published 1998
Copyright © Borough of Somerville, 1998

ISBN 0-7524-0878-X

Published by Arcadia Publishing,
an imprint of the Chalford Publishing Corporation,
One Washington Center, Dover, New Hampshire 03820.
Printed in Great Britain

Library of Congress Cataloging-in-Publication Data applied for

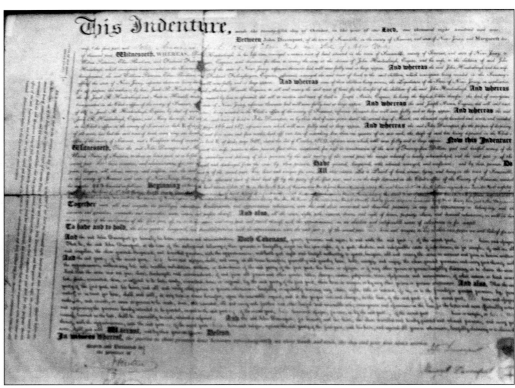

EARLY DEED, 1809. This document, transferring the title of property from John Hardenbergh to the Doughty family, is one of the earliest documents to use the name "Somerville" for the Raritan Valley village. The name is thought to have been in use since about 1800.

Contents

Acknowledgments 6

Introduction 7

1. Echoes of the Distant Past 9
2. Street Scenes and Landscapes 23
3. Notable Personalities and Famous Visitors 35
4. Pillars of the Community 49
5. Happenings and Disasters 67
6. In Case of Emergency 83
7. Commerce and Industry 93
8. Just Plain Folks 103
9. Home Sweet Home 117

Acknowledgments

Mayor David E. Hollod and our fellow committee members (David Hardgrove, Shirley Gurisic, Cathy Heath, William Lawton, Jeffrey Standing, the late Raymond Taub, and Randall Westbrook) have our gratitude for their enthusiastic endorsement of this project. We thank the Somerville Public Library for providing the core collection of photographs as well as work space and technical support. Special thanks go to Ms. Robin Feibush of Somerset County Library, Ms. Jessie Havens, and Mr. Walter Studdiford, who suggested sources and reference material, as well as to Elks Lodge #1068 for sharing their history with us. Ms. Sharon Wilson assisted with photographic copies and with cemetery photos. The Somerville and Old Raritan Cemetery Associations graciously permitted photography. We especially thank the following organizations and individuals who generously loaned photographs: Somerset County Historical Society (SCHS); the Firemen's Museum (FM); Somerville Board of Education (BOE); the *Somerset Messenger Gazette* (SMG); Somerset Medical Center (SMC); Branchburg Historical Society (BHS); the Somerset County Chapter of the American Red Cross; the U.S. Post Office, Somerville (USPO); Special Collections and Archives, Rutgers University Libraries; the Historical Photograph Collection, Alumnae Series, Princeton University Archives, Department of Rare Books and Special Collections, Princeton University Library (DRB/PUL); Oberlin College Archives, Oberlin, Ohio (OCA); Mr. W.J. Kurzenberger, New Jersey Division of Parks and Forestry; the John Kuhl Collection; Stevenson-D'Alessio VFW Post; Somerset County Cultural and Heritage Commission (CCHS); E. Boughner; Virginia Meredith Conard; Alvin Falk; Evelyn Field; Anna Goode; Virginia Demaray Gelin; Peter Grief; Anna Mae Hicks; Alice Higbee; Bill Hundley; Barry Jacobsen; Virginia Morneault; Barbara Navatto; Barbara Northrup; Mrs. George T. Oxford; Dorothy Stratford; Ann Sutphen; Julia Thompson; George and Henrietta Thomson; Rev. Pat Webster; Peter Wildgen; and Lillian Wissert.

Finally, apologies for any errors that may have crept into this work. As for omissions, a complete history of Somerville has yet to be written!

SOUTHERN SKYLINE, 1844.

Introduction

Somerville began over two centuries ago as an unincorporated village within Bridgewater Township. Settlers began carving homesteads out of "the Raritan Lots" around 1683. The first inhabitants were primarily Dutch colonials and their servants. Peter Van Neste, for whom Peter's Brook is named, first settled a tract that is now part of Somerville. The brook is probably named for him because he operated a gristmill along its banks. From just a few houses and an inn clustered at a crossroads in the late 1700s, Somerville became a bustling commercial and civic center of the early twentieth century. This volume showcases events and people in Somerville up to the decade following the First World War. It includes the earliest images of borough life through the Roaring Twenties. The photographs show a lively and diverse community.

The town was first a stagecoach stop. The area's major colonial roads, Old York Road, Easton Turnpike, and Old Pluckemin Road, shaped the small Raritan Valley village. Old York Road carried travelers through Somerville from the New York ferry to the Delaware crossing en route to Philadelphia. Excellent access to supplies and easy views of British movements from the nearby Watchung Hills led George Washington to make his winter camp here in 1778–79. After the British burned the church and the county courthouse on the nearby Millstone River, Cornelius Tunison donated land near his inn for new construction. From the 1790s, courthouse, church, and inn have presided over Main Street. The use of the name Somerville dates from this period, although the exact date and derivation of the name are unknown.

After 1842, the railroad transformed the small town, bringing industry and businessmen from the city. Charmed by the countryside, many built large, gracious homes typical of the Gilded Age. Local industry and rail access continued to draw a diverse population and varied interests. By the late 1800s, Somerville was a center of commerce, education, and the social scene—the heart of Somerset County. In 1862, a town charter was drawn up. A locally elected board of commissioners administered the town, although it was still part of the larger township. Civic pride and a sense that Somerville should determine its own course finally led to formal incorporation in 1909.

In the early years of this century, trolleys rolled along Somerville's Main Street carrying locals to its fine shopping district, factories, and businesses in its small but busy downtown. Before long, automobiles made their appearance on Main Street. This new mode of travel, the transformation of unpaved roads into modern highways and streets, and Somerville's central location reinforced its role as a regional center. As Somerville approaches its 90th anniversary, we hope its remarkable past will inspire its future as a crossroads of modern New Jersey.

Margaret Wolan Sullivan and the Book Committee: Virginia Gelin, Roberta Karpinecz, Mary Ellen Marsjanik, and Chairman James L. Sommerville

Councilwoman: Roberta Karpinecz

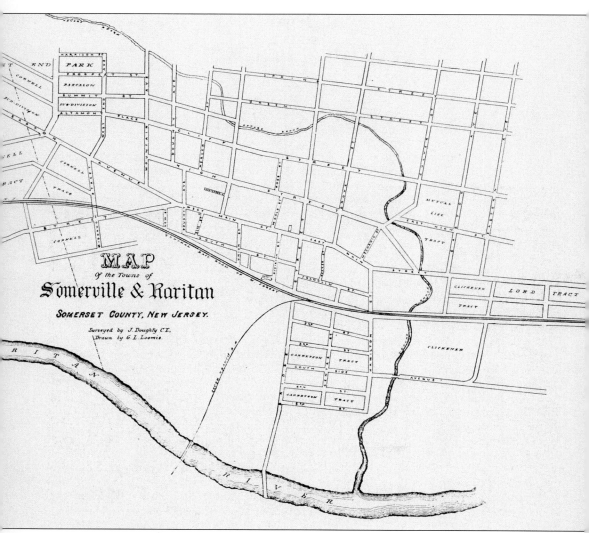

SOMERVILLE AND RARITAN, C. 1891. This map, surveyed by Joshua Doughty and drafted by George Loomis, was published in a photojournal of businesses and homes. Authors W. Parker and Joseph S. Frelinghuysen were actively recruiting businesses and developers. Somerville, with its railroad and stage connections, had grown more prosperous.

One
Echoes of the Distant Past

OLD DUTCH PARSONAGE. The Dutch Reformed Church was pivotal in the area's beginning. The original parsonage still stands as a symbol of Somerville's earliest history. Located on Washington Place, the Parsonage was built in 1751 for the Reverend John Frelinghuysen. It represents both the town's origins and the founding of Queens College, today known as Rutgers University.

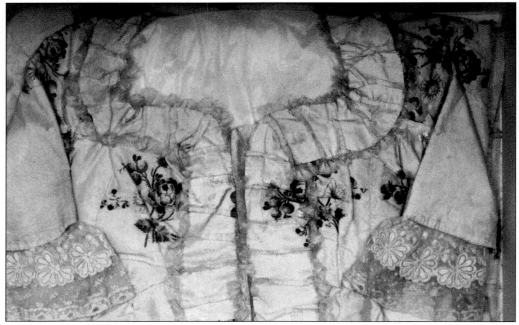

DINAH FRELINGHUYSEN HARDENBERGH'S (1725–1807) GOWN. The personality of Reverend Frelinghuysen's widow, who later became the wife of Reverend Hardenbergh, is reflected in this elegant gown preserved in Rutgers University's Special Collections. Mrs. Hardenbergh may have worn it while entertaining at the Parsonage. The gown's style was fashionable in the mid-1700s. (SCHS.)

MAJOR GENERAL FREDERICK FRELINGHUYSEN (1753–1804). Born and raised at the Parsonage, Frelinghuysen was one of New Jersey's most distinguished patriots. In this late-1790s portrait, he wears the Society of the Cincinnati's medal for exemplary service during the American Revolution. He was Queens College's first instructor and later served as a Congressional delegate, county clerk, and U.S. senator. (Courtesy of J. Kurzenberger, State Park Service.)

JACOB RUSTEN HARDENBERGH (1736–1790). Among the young men trained for the ministry at the Old Dutch Parsonage, Hardenbergh became the first minister of the First Reformed Church ordained in America, and he returned to the Parsonage as Frelinghuysen's successor. A founder and later president of Queens College, Hardenbergh served New Jersey as a Provincial Assembly delegate and voted to ratify the Declaration of Independence. (Special Collections and University Archives, Rutgers University Libraries.)

LOTTERY TICKETS. After the Revolution, the First Reformed congregation raised funds for building a new church by holding a lottery. The British had burnt the original structure in 1779. Dated 1793, these tickets were signed by Frederick Frelinghuysen, who served as a lottery manager. Over 5,500 tickets were sold at $2 each. The successful endeavor led to the building of a new church in Somerville on land donated by Cornelius Tunison.

John Wallace (1717–1783). Upon retiring from the Philadelphia City Council and the textile trade, this Scotsman purchased property in what became Somerville. He built his country home sometime before 1777. A man of business, Wallace negotiated a fee for the use of his house during the 1778–79 Middlebrook encampment. It would be the only time George Washington paid rent for his headquarters. (Courtesy of J. Kurzenberger, State Park Service.)

Mary Maddox Wallace (1732–1784). Little is known about Wallace's wife. However, mention of her name in a letter written by George Washington verified local lore when this correspondence was discovered more than a century later. Washington wrote that he was staying at "Mrs. Wallis' [sic] house, about 12 miles from New Brunswick." (Courtesy of J. Kurzenberger, State Park Service.)

THE WALLACE HOUSE, C. 1897. A citizens' group, led by Prudential executive Richard Stevens, raised funds to preserve the former Wallace home. Calling themselves the Revolutionary Memorial Society, the group maintained the site as a headquarters and museum until turning it over to the State in 1948. This front view appeared in the dedication program. The Victorian porch was not original and has since been removed.

THE WALLACE HOUSE PASSAGE, C. 1905. This view of the central hall of the Wallace House looks toward the front door. The hand-hewn arch is shown as well as some of the artifacts collected by the Revolutionary Memorial Society. The house interior remains relatively unchanged since Washington's time. The Miller family, who owned the house and farm for most of the 1800s, made only minor renovations.

ABRAHAM TUNISON HEADSTONE, 1797. This stone and others in a small family graveyard mark the final resting places of several early families, including the Strykers, Beekmans, Tunisons, Vanderveers, and Comptons. The Tunisons are one of Somerville's "founding" families, and successive generations were prominent leaders in the local Dutch Reformed Church. The family also opened an inn at the crossroads sometime prior to 1770.

A PRESERVATION MOVEMENT, 1913. When progress demanded regrading of the railroad bed, the Old Dutch Parsonage was preserved by relocating it to Washington Place. No photo of the actual move exists, but five other houses were similarly relocated by the Cott-A-Lapp Company. Pictured here is one of these houses as it is slid across the rails to its new location, most likely today's No. 41–43 Washington Place.

STRYKER'S LICENSE, 1790. New Jersey was the first colony to require licensing of physicians (1772). Dr. Peter Stryker, who made the Parsonage his residence sometime after 1810, may have been Somerville's first doctor. Besides medical practice, Stryker had several business interests and was active in politics. He served terms as county sheriff and vice president of the state senate. (SCHS.)

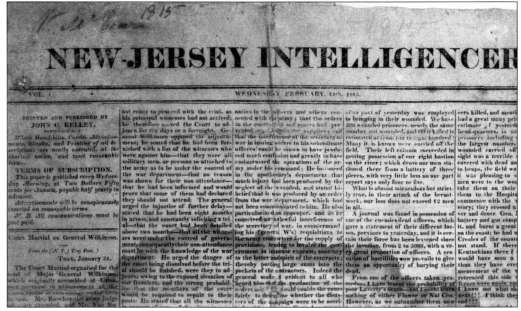

THE NEW JERSEY INTELLIGENCER, 1815 EDITION. Information on day-to-day life in early Somerville is known through its newspapers. At one time, the town boasted three such publications. First printed about 1814, the *New Jersey Intelligencer* was Somerville's first newspaper. (SCHS.)

PETER VROOM'S OFFICE. Pictured is the original front entry of 48 East Main, the former law office of Peter Vroom, Somerville's most famous citizen prior to the Civil War. Vroom was twice a governor of New Jersey and the U.S. minister to the Prussian Court from 1854 to 1857. The structure later housed the Somerville Athletic Club and eventually Somerville Aluminum. (SCHS.)

STAGE ADVERTISEMENT, 1840. Somerville was a stagecoach stop throughout the 1800s. Two independent lines connected at the hotel on Grove and Main Streets. John Argue's line carried travelers from New York via New Brunswick for a 50¢ fare. The Swift-Sure Stage line ran from Newark via Somerville to the Lambertville ferry—then onward to Philadelphia. George Layton operated the stage between Somerville and Peapack until 1911. (SMG.)

FARE FROM New-York to Somerville reduced to 50 Cents.

NEW-JERSEY RAIL-ROAD LINE.

J. ARGUE'S STAGE.

THIS Stage hereafter will run as follows: Leave Torbert's Hotel, (calling at Fritts' Hotel,) at 5½ and 10½ A. M., affording passengers an opportunity of going to New-York with the first train of Cars, and at 12 1-2 P. M.—also affording Passengers for Princeton, Trenton and Philadelphia, who take the first stage, a speedy conveyance to either of said places.

Returning, leave the Raritan House, New-Brunswick, (calling at Joline's and the Rail Road Depot,) at 11 A. M. and at 7 P. M.—after the arrival of the Cars.

☞ Passengers will bear in mind, that the Office in N. York, is at the foot of Liberty-street, where they must be particular to have their names entered on the Somerville Way Bill, otherwise they will be charged the regular fare from N. Brunswick. The cars that connect with this line leave N. York at 9 A. M. and ¼ before 5 P. M.

This Stage intersects the Swiftsure Stage Line at Somerville on Mondays, Wednesdays and Fridays. Passengers who take the 9 o'clock cars from New-York on either of the above days, can be conveyed immediately to Centreville, Flemington, Lambertville, or any of the intermediate places along that route.

JOHN ARGUE.

Somerville, May 1, 1840.   53

FRANKLIN AGRICULTURAL SOCIETY!

The Fair of the Season
AT SOMERVILLE, N. J.
OCTOBER the 2nd, 3rd, 4th and 5th, 1860

Ladies are cordially invited to contribute; Farmers, Manufacturers, Stock-Raisers a[nd] Horsemen from every part of the Union are invited to bring articles to this Exhibition. [So]me of the fastest Trotting Horses in the U. States will be here, and all who wish to see the best [of] Trotting will be gratified, as we have the best **Track** in the country, and pay the most and highest **Premiu**[ms of] [an]y Society in New Jersey.

To prevent confusion and want of time, as there will be a large lot of Stock to examine, the Judges are par[ticularly] requested to commence their duties on WEDNESDAY, so as to give entire satisfaction to all.

ORDER OF EXERCISES.

BROADSIDE, 1860. An agricultural fair is still an end-of-summer tradition in Somerset County. In the 1800s, Somerville was the site of these agricultural fairs. The events were sponsored by the Central New Jersey Railroad, a shipper of local produce and a major exhibitor. To promote the fairs and their own business, the railroad provided discounted tickets to those traveling by train. Once there, fair-goers could enjoy events such as trotter races, popular since Dutch colonial times.

CAMMANN'S CASTLE. This daguerreotype of 45 West End Avenue is probably the earliest photographic image of Somerville. Albert Cammann, owner of local copper mines, built this brooding Gothic structure about 1842. Reportedly, it was the first house in town with indoor plumbing. In 1888, a new owner demolished the castle and replaced it with another edifice, known since 1958 as Somerville's Borough Hall. (SCHS.)

JOHN H. VANDERVEER. One of many Somerville men who volunteered during the Civil War, Vanderveer joined Company E of the 15th New Jersey Infantry in 1862. Attaining the rank of captain, he was wounded in 1864 at the Wilderness battle and discharged with a disabled hand. Vanderveer became a clerk of the state senate but died of a sudden illness in 1869. This *carte de visite* was taken by Mathew Brady Studios. (Courtesy of the John Kuhl Collection.)

ARABELLA W. GRIFFITH BARLOW (1824–1864). A Somerville native, the wife of Union General Francis Barlow was a civilian nurse caring for the wounded during the Peninsula, Antietam, and Gettysburg campaigns. This unsung Civil War heroine died from typhus contracted while in the service of her country and humanity. A plaque erected in 1996 at the base of Barlow's headstone pays tribute to her extraordinary deeds.

JAMES SUYDAM KNOX, 1860. A local doctor in later years, young Knox enjoyed the theater. On April 14, 1865, he attended a soon-to-become infamous production at Ford's Theater in Washington D.C. There he witnessed President Abraham Lincoln's assassination. Knox unsuccessfully pursued John Wilkes Booth on the theater's darkened backstage. He described these events in a letter to his father, which is preserved at Princeton University. (DRB/PUL.)

U.S. COLORED INFANTRY. Among the Civil War veterans buried in Somerville are members of the U.S. Colored Infantry. This headstone is unusual; its owner was prosperous enough to purchase his marker from the Grand Army of the Republic, a Civil War veterans' association. Typically small, white, army-issue stones bearing the initials, U.S.C. Inf., give testimony to the fight of local freemen for their countrymen's liberty.

1873 STEAM PUMPER ON PARADE. Recapturing an earlier era, antique fire-fighting equipment went on parade for the 1935 centennial of Somerville's volunteer fire department. Pictured is the department's original steam-powered pumper as it passes before the reviewing stand in front of the county courthouse. The pumper, which cost $5,000 when new, remains on display at the Fireman's Museum on Doughty Street.

GRADUATION PROGRAM, 1889.
Somerville's public high school opened its doors in 1886 with a two-year course of study. This program from the second commencement lists 12 graduates, including one who was awarded his diploma posthumously. Peter Melick Van Cleef was class valedictorian. Graduation was held in the Armory Hall on Main Street for years because the school had no auditorium.

PHOTOGRAPHER'S AD, C. 1895. The Somerville Merchants Association, forerunner of the Chamber of Commerce, compiled and donated a "Business Look Me Through" to the Public Library. The album contains hand-drawn and colored advertisements of Somerville businesses of the era. Howard's Studio on Main Street probably produced the project. The studio no doubt was also noted for its photography as evidenced by this portrait of an unidentified little miss.

THE LORD FOUNTAIN. Shown shortly after construction in 1909, this marble fountain, dedicated to John Haynes Lord, graced the unpaved corner of Main and Grove. The 1908 county jail can be seen in the background. Designed by architect John Russell Pope, the fountain was donated by Lord's sister for the benefit of "man and beast." Horseless carriages soon left the fountain without function. The basin last held water in 1933. (BHS.)

VOTES FOR WOMEN. Suffragettes campaigned vigorously during the summer of 1915 for the state suffrage referendum, pitching their tent on the courthouse green. Mayor Steele and his sister Mary, the first woman admitted to the state's bar, supported the referendum. But Somerville did not share their enthusiasm. The town joined other New Jersey towns in barring women from the polling place until the passage of federal suffrage amendment in 1921. (FM.)

Two
Street Scenes and Landscapes

TRAIN STATION, C. 1900. Often a bustling place at the turn of the last century, this sandstone station was built in 1890. Constructed of rusticated stone from the Stockton quarries, it was designed for the Central Railroad of New Jersey by architect Frank Bodine. This photo depicts a typical track-side scene as travelers gather at this important and stylish transportation center.

ALTAMONT PLACE, C. 1909. Somerville has a fine stock of Victorian architecture. This postcard illustrates a few of Somerville's finest late-Victorian homes, looking west from the Mountain Avenue intersection. J. Harper Smith's mansion is second from the corner.

SOMERSET STREET, C. 1900. This trolley, on its Raritan–Bound Brook run, trundles up the Somerset Street hill just beyond the Central New Jersey Railroad overpass. Trolleys operated in town for a relatively short time. The first tracks were first laid down in Somerville in 1894. Trains were discontinued in 1927, but the tracks remained until they were recycled as scrap metal in World War II.

PETER'S BROOK, C. 1905. Named for one of Somerville's first settlers, the brook and adjacent parks have provided a slice of country in a small-town environment for decades. The parks were officially preserved in the 1930s through the vision and efforts of Mayor Thomas Flockhart. These early postcards show the natural, wild beauty of the stream and its surroundings.

BRIDGE STREET, C. 1905. This postcard provides a glimpse of the west side of Bridge Street, looking southwest from Peter's Brook. These comfortable, early-twentieth-century gable-front houses can still be seen and for the most part have remained true to their original style.

MAIN STREET SOUTH, C. 1921. This southern view of Main Street, looking west from the corner of Bridge and West Main, depicts the Second National Bank (Fleet Bank) and adjacent buildings. Wearing its patriotic best, Somerville waited for President Warren G. Harding to sign the treaty ending World War I. He did so a few miles west of this location.

THE "GASTON" BUILDING, C. 1900. This is a fine close-up of the Romanesque brownstone structure on the corner of Main and Maple. Built by Senator Lewis Thompson in 1891, it became known locally by the name of the store occupying the ground floor. John G. Gaston's name is visible on the awning. In addition to the department store, the building housed the Somerville Post Office at the turn of the century. (SMG.)

MAIN STREET LOOKING WEST, C. 1909. This view of Main Street shows Somerville at the dawn of the auto age. Horse-drawn carriages, automobiles, and trolleys shared the thoroughfare passing in front of the First National Bank and the Gaston building. The flag proudly waving from the turret of the Gaston building, as well as several others displayed at street level among the awnings, suggests a patriotic occasion. (SMG.)

MAIN STREET, C. 1900. This view of the north side of Main Street shows the variety of stores present in town at the turn of the century. Among other businesses, Somerville boasted a sewing notions shop, a drugstore, shoe store, and a carpet and dry goods store, as shown left to right in this photo. This building still stands, but the street level shops have been modernized.

59–61 WEST MAIN STREET, C. 1885. The original Gernert's Store on Main Street was essentially a "general store" offering a variety of stock including children's items such as the Champion wagon, go-cart, tricycles, and toys (a sailboat is in the window along with teacups). Gernert's remained a Somerville shop until the 1990s.

GROVE AND MAIN, C. 1890. After passing through several owners, Tunison's tavern became the Fritts' Hotel in 1847. Enlarged a few times by owner Jacob A. Fritts, the hotel included a two-story wing that had been Tunison's original inn. Throughout the late 1800s, the hotel remained an upscale establishment. Local politicians often gathered at Fritts' for meetings. (SCHS.)

SOMERSET HOTEL, C. 1908. When the courthouse was constructed, new owners made major renovations to the old hotel. Much of Fritts' Hotel, including its oldest wing, was demolished. Despite the extensive remodeling, the hotel was never closed, making it the oldest continuously operating hotel in the United States. Reconstructed in Colonial Spanish, or "Mission" style, it again offered first-class accommodations.

STRYKER'S CORNER, C. 1900. This view of the corner of Grove and Main predates the construction of the 1907 courthouse and Lord Fountain, which later occupied this site. A house stood on this location since at least 1857, although Mr. Stryker (second from right) did not always own the property. A.J. Van Fleet, far right, is also identified in the photo.

CLASSIC ROADSTER, 1921. License plate #7490 parked on Main Street in front of the courthouse—note the crumpled fender marking an unexpected encounter. Warren Street is in the left background. Across the street from the Central Garage is the "new" Unionist-Gazette building. Next door, the gate of the Vanderveer home is curiously open—Mrs. Vanderveer routinely locked it to keep passing schoolchildren from picking her violets. (SMG.)

WARREN STREET, 1920. Checking out the latest in commercial transportation, these men take a break in front of the Central Garage at Main and Warren Streets. While J.C. Henry's garage hummed with mechanical activity on the first floor, a pool hall on the second floor helped pass some leisure time.

MAIN STREET, C. 1900. This view of Main, looking toward Division Street, appears in Harry Berd's Somerville panorama. Many of the pictured buildings and businesses no longer exist. Ten Eyck Hotel with its distinctive wrought-iron balcony stands at the corner of Division Street. It opened in Somerville before the Civil War. Visible at mid-block is the tiny office of the *Somerset Messenger*, a forerunner of the *Messenger-Gazette*. (SMG.)

DAVENPORT AND WEST MAIN, C. 1900. Most likely on a return run to the firehouse, West End Company's horse-drawn hose truck passes the intersection of Davenport Street. Acquired in 1899, the rig had rubber tires and was considered quite modern. Driver John Crollman holds Mackey's reins—Mackey was the first horse owned by the Somerville Fire Department. Prior to his purchase, all equipment was hand-hauled.

EAST END GROCERY, C. 1900. Before the days of supermarket chains, many neighborhood grocery stores operated in Somerville. Wearing a white duster coat, proprietor William Hamilton greets customers in front of his establishment. The East End Grocery was located on the corner of Warren and Main and had considerable competition. Eleven groceries and dry goods shops were listed in the 1890 business directory.

4–6 West Main, c. 1910. Alpaugh and La Roe combined a grocery with a butcher's shop. They were also apparently supporters of the public library. A poster invites patrons to visit the store "early and often" to vote in a library-sponsored contest.

Hardgrove and Kline, c. 1918. Located on the south side of Main Street, this building's cast-iron storefront made it one of the more unique downtown structures. It was demolished during urban renewal in the 1970s. Dressed patriotically, the building is probably decorated in honor of Independence or Armistice Day around the time of the First World War.

REGENT THEATER, C. 1916. Somerville's Regent Theater offered vaudeville and the best of the silent screen, adding to the leisure time activities available in town. The theater opened in this Main Street building in the early 1900s. Ready for a busy evening, the staff awaits its patrons. In the background, movie posters announce coming attractions.

THEATER STAFF, C. 1916. The theater staff poses good naturedly before showtime. From left to right are as follows: Mr. Kellar, custodian; Mr. Girade, manager; and Miss Carson, cashier. The final couple is identified as "the Peanut Operators." In the background, posters for current silent film attractions, including a Keystone Cop comedy, are visible.

Three
Notable Personalities and Famous Visitors

WAITING FOR THE PRESIDENT, C. 1921. Filled with anticipation, a huge crowd gathered at the train station to greet the Chief Executive. A favorite stop for presidents and presidents-to-be, Somerville hosted Ulysses S. Grant, Chester Arthur, Grover Cleveland, Teddy Roosevelt, Howard Taft, Woodrow Wilson, and Warren G. Harding. The tradition began more than two centuries ago when future first president George Washington stayed at the Wallace House. (FM.)

GENERAL GEORGE WASHINGTON. The general was perhaps Somerville's most distinguished visitor. No stranger to New Jersey, Washington made his "Camp Middlebrook" headquarters at the Wallace House in 1778. The Commander-in-chief was about 45 years old at the time. This pen and ink sketch of Washington appeared in the 1897 dedication program of the Wallace House Museum.

WILLIAM JENNINGS BRYAN, 1908. Democratic presidential candidate Bryan drew a large crowd during his Somerville whistle stop on October 23, 1908. Before the days of mass media, the train brought presidential campaigns to the doorsteps of local residents. It was the third presidential run for the great American orator. Known as "the Great Commoner," Bryan promoted himself as a man of the people and a true representative of their interests.

THEODORE ROOSEVELT, 1912. The former President stumped in Somerville as the Bull Moose Party candidate. Greeted enthusiastically at the train station, Teddy shook hands before heading to the courthouse. There he gave a stirring speech on the courthouse steps in the typical Roosevelt style. Despite the interest he generated, he did not enjoy victory. Neither New Jersey nor the rest of America was ready to elect a third party president.

WOODROW WILSON POLITICAL CARTOON, 1915. The *Unionist Gazette* ran this cartoon, paid for by the New Jersey Equal Suffrage Committee, during the state's suffrage campaign. Although former governor Wilson retained his New Jersey voter registration, his personal popularity did not help the cause. Somerville joined every other municipality in the county, except for Montgomery and Rocky Hill, in refusing woman's suffrage until the passage of the federal amendment in 1920. (SMG.)

SHAKING HANDS WITH THE PRESIDENT, c. 1912. The crowd rushes the grandstand in order to be able to shake hands with President Taft during his visit. (SCHS.)

HARDING, THE GOLFER, C. 1921. President Warren G. Harding was an avid golfer. He was the guest of Senator Joseph S. Frelinghuysen at the Raritan Valley Country Club on July 2, 1921. He was relaxing on the links when word was telegraphed that a courier would arrive with a treaty for his signature. (FM.)

KNOX-PORTER COMMEMORATIVE POSTCARD. World War I officially ended for America on July 2, 1921, when President Harding signed the Knox-Porter Resolution, as shown in this postcard issued and postmarked from the Somerville Post Office. Although the signing technically occurred in Raritan, it was less than a mile from Somerville. The borough was strongly identified with the event.

EUGENE S. DOUGHTY (1812–1888). The Doughty brothers were successful and prominent businessmen of the Victorian Era. Younger brother Eugene owned a lumberyard on the future site of Somerville's textile mill and lace works at Doughty and New Streets. He also served in the New Jersey Assembly. (SCHS.)

JOSHUA DOUGHTY SR. (1799–1881). Joshua, the elder Doughty, ran a general store in the first brick building on Main Street and later became president of the first local bank. Elected to the state senate in 1863, Joshua was also president of Somerville's first board of education. He established a free, graded public school years before the state's 1875 school mandate. (SCHS.)

THE LADIES OF THE DOUGHTY CLAN, C. 1892. The wife and daughter of Joshua Doughty Sr. entertain friends in a fashionable "surrey with the fringe on top." Miss Louisa Doughty later married into the Cammann family, who were the original owners of the Borough Hall property. (SCHS.)

HARPER SMITH MONUMENT. Wealthy businessman James Harper Smith (1834–1911) was partner and manager of the Raritan Woolen Mills. A patron of the arts, "Super" Smith engaged noted architect Horace Trumbauer to design his personal library and St. John's Episcopal Church, as well as houses for two of his executives. Commissioned on the death of his only son in 1907, Smith's "Angel of Peace" monument reflects his aesthetic tastes and enduring faith.

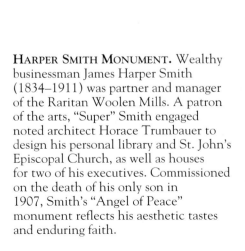

Antoinne L. Brown Blackwell, c. 1847. This Oberlin College graduate became the first American woman ordained as a Protestant minister. She did not preach in Somerville, but wrote several books while raising her family here. She and her husband, brother of Dr. Elizabeth Blackwell, were charter members of the Monday Evening Club. Advocates of women's suffrage, they were probably instrumental in bringing Susan B. Anthony to lecture in Somerville in 1872. (OCA.)

Abraham Van Doren Honeyman, c. 1879. Assuming the editorship before his 30th birthday, Honeyman ran the *Unionist Gazette*, a predecessor of the *Messenger-Gazette*. He also left Somerville the legacy of the Monday Evening Club. At his instigation, a group of local residents with common interests in literature and current events began meeting weekly. The club has met regularly for over 100 years. (SMG.)

DR. MARY GASTON, C. 1915. Graduating in 1888 from Women's Medical College in Philadelphia, Mary Gaston returned to Somerville to become the county's first woman physician. A philanthropist and activist, she founded Somerville's Civic League and was a benefactor of the library and hospital. Although a heart attack forced her into early retirement in 1907 at age 55, this active and vital woman lived to be 100 years of age. (SCHS).

HUGH K. GASTON (1858–1938). "HK," as he was known, was one of the county's leading lawyers and a benefactor of local organizations, especially the library. He had no children of his own, but personally did much for youth. Several young men attended college through his generosity. His Cliff Street home was a prime stop on Halloween. It was one of the few dispensing candy, which was expensive in those days.

JOSEPHINE BIGGS HAMILTON, C. 1920. Serving from approximately 1911 to 1924, Mrs. Hamilton was Somerset Hospital's first superintendent, head of nursing, and director of the first nursing school. Also as the school's main instructor, she developed the nursing curriculum. A nurse's life, she wrote, is "governed by military precision . . . her's is a life of self-sacrifice." Her sudden, untimely death from a stroke in 1924 left many of her projects unfinished.

CHARLES C. KENYON, C. 1909. Somerville's first mayor owned a local textile firm and held a U.S. patent for machinery equipment invented at the plant. Running under the banner, "Time for Change," Kenyon led the campaign to incorporate Somerville. It was the right theme for a new century. A major turning point, the referendum passed 450-138 in 1908, receiving final legislative approval on April 16, 1909.

RUTH ST. DENIS, C. 1910. Known for modern dance, St. Denis studied with Somerville's Miss Maude Davenport as a young girl. While still in school, she made her stage debut at Main Street's Somerset Hall. Although Ruth left for New York City at age 15, residents remembered her fondly. This print is from an original glass negative. It was a gift many years ago to a devoted fan of the celebrated dancer.

ANNA CASE. Somerville nurtured another star—Metropolitan Opera singer and concert soloist Anna Case. A native of South Branch, this blacksmith's daughter studied with Catherine Updyck. She was just 21 when "discovered." Known around the world, Case married multi-millionaire postal and telegraph magnate Clarence Mackay.

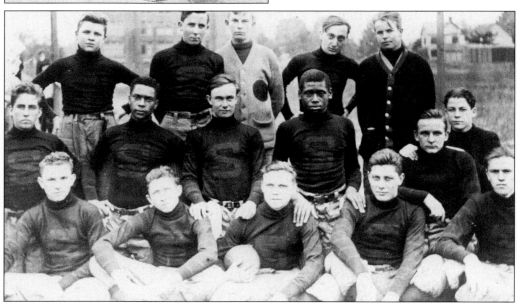

PIONEER FOOTBALL TEAM, 1913. This cherished photograph of Somerville High's football team was contributed by the family of Arthur I. Meredith (holding the ball), on whose shoulder Paul Robeson's (second row, center) hand gently rests. Both boys were sophomores in the Class of 1915. Other identified teammates are as follows: Amerman (second row, far left); Moreland Douglas, Class of 1916 (second row, second from left); and McHugh (on Meredith's right).

SHERRILL BABCOCK RICHARDS

"Virtuous and vicious every man must be,
Few in th' extreme, but all in the degree."

Clerk of Commission; Senior Play; Glee Club.—Lehigh.

PAUL LEROY ROBESON

"Doing all with a deal of skill."

School Orator; Debating Team; Athletic Editor Valkyrie; Senior Play; Glee Club; "S" F. B. (4), B. B. (4), Bk. B. (3).—Honorman—Rutgers.

JOHN JACOB SCHOMP

"Windy in running, but not in talking."

Glee Club. "S" Track (3), B. B. (4).

RUDOLPH SCHWOERER

"Too lately and too little known."

VALKYRIE, 1915. Paul Robeson was listed with fellow seniors in Somerville High's yearbook. His remarkable list of accomplishments hinted of greatness to come. A lawyer, singer, actor, and social activist, Robeson became the most widely known and controversial civil rights advocate of the early twentieth century. He lived and grew to adulthood in Somerville.

JOHN ROWLAND STEVENSON, C. 1917. A fresh-faced young man went off to war in 1916 but did not return. He was killed in the Argonne Forest in 1918, a few weeks shy of Armistice Day. Originally laid to rest in France, his coffin was returned home for re-internment. His body lay in state in the rotunda of the courthouse, and was subsequently buried with full military honors on Armistice Day, 1921. (VFW.)

FOUNDER OF SHILOH PENTECOSTAL CHURCH. Arriving in Somerville in 1929, Mother Ruth Brown began holding services in the living room of her home on Davenport Street. Under her leadership, a new congregation broke ground for the church on the corner of Green and Davenport Streets shortly after World War II. Here, she celebrates an anniversary with her successors, the Reverends Denvil and Adeline Harley.

Four
Pillars of the Community

DISMISSAL TIME, C. 1910. Some things never seem to change. The bell rings and children dash out of Somerville's first public elementary school building to continue their afternoon at play. This familiar scene and others in this chapter reflect the themes of life and the continuity of the Somerville community.

FIRST PUBLIC SCHOOL, 1900. Erected around 1856, Somerville's first public school began as a square brick building but later underwent expansion to meet growing community needs. Shown here in 1900, the school had 12 rooms and no gymnasium. "Boys only" attended as late as 1882. The high school occupied one room on the top floor. (SCHS.)

BOYS' SCHOOL CALENDAR, C. 1881. This calendar for the Grammar School for Boys sets the agenda for the academic year. Boarding students were accepted, but they had to supply their own linens. The fee schedule lists the costs for an education in the late 1800s. A private preparatory school and young ladies "seminary" also existed in Somerville during the early 1800s.

BREAKING NEW GROUND IN EDUCATION, C. 1922. Local dignitaries proudly break ground for Somerville's "new" high school. Turning the shovels at the Cliff Street site are, from left to right, as follows: Bill Kirby, T. Latimer Brooks (school superintendent), Adolph Merthens, Dr. Wallace Naylor, Aylin Pierson, Mrs. Ezra Weldon, Oliver Allen, Mrs. Alice Cornelison, B.L. Wharton, Jacob Brokaw, W.V. Purcell, and George Nevius. The completed structure eventually became Somerville Middle School. Brooks Field, the high school's athletic field, is named for the superintendent. (BOE.)

FIRST HIGH SCHOOL, C. 1904. Somerville's first separate high school building featured a dedicated assembly room, the first for the district. At the rear is the original grammar school edifice that connected to the new facility. This attractive building may seem vaguely familiar. Although lacking in some of its original design details, it now serves as the board of education's headquarters.

LAFAYETTE ELEMENTARY SCHOOL, C. 1908. A growing population on the town's east end led to the construction of the Lafayette School at Gaston Avenue and High Street. The opening of a fourth school also marked the town's second expansion in ten years. Named for the French Revolutionary War hero who had visited Washington at the Wallace House, the building was used as a school until 1980; it now serves as an office building.

OLD FIRST REFORMED CHURCH, C. 1888. Established in 1699, the First Reformed congregation is the oldest Christian denomination in the area. The congregation has made its home in Somerville since the 1780s. It relocated to the town green after the original church, built near the river, was burned during the American Revolution. This brick structure replaced an earlier wooden church in 1834. This edifice, in turn, was torn down to allow construction of a new house of worship in 1897. The small building on the right was part of the county complex that shared the green. (BHS.)

First Reformed Church, c. 1910. Designed by William Appleton Potter, the First Reformed congregation's new stone church seated 900 worshippers. "This is where I belong," wrote Mary Gaston. "Please hang on to it for me." She meant this postcard, but got her wish twice. Her family saved the postcard, and the beautiful Gothic church became the Jury Assembly Room in 1987. The First and Second Reformed Churches united in 1974.

St. John's Episcopal Church, c. 1906. Dedicated in 1896, this castellated church, designed by Horace Trumbauer, serves the Episcopal congregation. It replaced the church built on land donated by Joshua Doughty in 1851. The old church was moved to the rear of the lot, where it continued as a parish hall until 1925. The former carriage entrance to the stone church was transformed into a baptistery at the same time.

SECOND REFORMED CHURCHES (1834–1974). The Second Reformed congregation has had two churches. The first was a wooden frame church on Division Street. The dedication of the new Richardsonian Gothic church on Main Street in 1894 was a great occasion. (SCHS.)

SECOND REFORMED CHURCHES (1834–1974). Designed by Oscar Teal, the new house of worship is constructed of stone from the Martinsville quarries. The church now serves the United Reformed congregation.

IMMACULATE CONCEPTION CHURCH AND RECTORY, C. 1910. Dedicated in 1888, this small brick church on West High and Davenport housed Somerville's first Catholic parish, organized in 1882. Founding pastor Martin Von Den Bogaard resided in the rectory next door to the church. The former rectory still stands, but the church was destroyed by fire in 1965. Masses were celebrated in school gymnasiums until the new church complex on Mountain Avenue was dedicated in 1975.

FIRST BAPTIST CHURCH, 1906. In 1873, this High Street structure replaced the First Baptist congregation's meetinghouse on Main Street. Designed by Asa Dilts, a local builder who erected many New Jersey churches, it featured a spire with a clock (regarded by many as the town's "official" timepiece), as did its predecessor. In 1926, the clock, its spire, and much of the church were badly damaged by fire.

METHODIST EPISCOPAL CHURCH, 1906. This Gothic style church on West High replaced the congregation's original wooden building, built in 1832 on South Bridge Street. Only the 1893 parsonage remains on South Bridge, and it is used as a private residence. Following the unification of the Raritan and Somerville Methodist congregations in the mid-1920s, a third larger church was erected on this site and dedicated in 1929.

ST. THOMAS CHURCH, C. 1900. Organized in 1858, the African Methodist Episcopal Zion church on Davenport Street is the borough's oldest African-American Christian community. The congregation struggled for many years until it was able to construct this permanent house of worship on its own land. Paul Robeson worshiped at this church. His father relocated his family here when he assumed the pastorate in 1910.

ANSHE CHESED, C. 1910. Located on East Main, this synagogue was the first Jewish house of worship west of Plainfield. It served the community for nearly 50 years. Senator J.S. Frelinghuysen laid its cornerstone in 1909. The following fall, the Torah was carried in procession down Main Street from Germainia Hall, the congregation's first meeting place, to the new site. The structure currently serves the Covenant Missionary Baptist Church.

ST. PAUL BAPTIST CHURCH. Members of the congregation gather at their early meeting site on Hamilton Street. Begun as a mission, St. Paul was organized in 1927 with Joseph Aaron Lacey as pastor. The church still counts founding members among its congregation; almost certainly, many of them appear in this photo. The Hamilton Street site of the church was purchased in 1931.

ELKS' FIRST CLUBHOUSE, 1914. The former home of Dr. Wallace Naylor, this frame dwelling on Main Street served as the Elks' first clubhouse. Organized in 1907, the 22-member Somerville chapter began when an earlier men's social group, the Jolly Corks, affiliated with the national fraternal organization. Frederick Wink was the first Exalted Ruler of Lodge 1068, which is dedicated to helping disabled children and other charitable causes.

BANK AT MAPLE AND MAIN, 1901. Designed by George Post, architect of the New York Stock Exchange, this Beaux Arts style building has housed several different banks since its construction in 1900. A street clock was the only major exterior embellishment since its days as the First National Bank and later, Somerset Trust Company. The first Main Street offices of the Unionist Gazette Book and Job Printing stood next door. (SMG.)

Grove Street Armory, c. 1918. Decorated for the "Welcome Home" festivities at the end of the First World War, this simple brick edifice was home to Somerset County's Second National Guard Regiment. Open to the public since 1910, the Armory and its predecessor, a wooden frame structure on Somerset Street, known as Armory Hall, both served Somerville as a community gathering place for many years. Armory Hall was used for high school graduations in the early days of the public school. (FM.)

ARMORY, INSIDE VIEW. In this photo, the drill room is decorated for a Christmas party. Among the events held in the 1910 Armory were a suffrage rally (1915), the kick-off rally of the local chapter of the American Red Cross (1917), and a "Welcome Home" dinner/dance for returning veterans of World War I (1919). The building, lately used by the County Sheriff's Department, is scheduled for demolition by the County.

MAPLE STREET LIBRARY, 1902–1928. This small, yet striking, building was once the home of the Somerville Public Library. Designed by George W. Post, it was built expressly for the library, which rapidly outgrew the space. Operating continuously since 1871, the library was a citizen's association until 1912, when it was incorporated as a free library and became a borough service. The library and borough began sharing space in 1928.

LIBRARY INTERIOR, C. 1910. The interior of the library seems austere and low tech by today's standards, but it was, then as now, a quiet place to retreat for reading and stretching the mind. A prominently located clock helped patrons from losing track of time.

Schwed Mansion, c. 1929. Formerly home to the Schwed family, this Italianate brick mansion on the corner of Bridge and High Streets became home to the borough and the library in 1928. With the library on the first floor and borough offices on the second, it also housed the police station. Charles Schwed, merchant and member of the first Borough Council, operated a clothing store on Main Street in the late 1800s.

THE ROBERT MANSION, 1891. Once the private residence of Daniel Robert, this Gothic home is a copy of a famous Bridgeport mansion originally designed by noted architect Alexander Jackson Davis. Building in 1888, Robert used the same architectural firm that had remodeled the original mansion in order to produce a faithful copy. The Bridgeport home was demolished in 1958, but Robert's copy survived. It became the Elks' second clubhouse from 1923 to 1927. An impressive reminder of a bygone era, it has become the home of borough offices and the library.

BANKS ON BRIDGE AND MAIN. A bank on this corner has been a landmark since at least 1857. The structure with its iron grates (shown above) was constructed first. A Somerville landmark since its construction in 1914, the Second National Bank (shown below)—now Fleet Bank—was designed by local architect Jay C. Van Nuys. Van Nuys's firm, a predecessor of Shive, Spinelli, Perantoni and Associates, still has offices in town.

OLD COURTHOUSE, C. 1898. Built in 1799, Somerset County's third courthouse replaced two earlier wooden buildings that were destroyed by fire. The simple brick structure was enlarged in 1849 by adding another story and a temple-style portico, as shown. The two small buildings on either side housed the county clerk's and the surrogate's offices. All were demolished in 1906 to make way for a new courthouse.

COURTHOUSE UNDER CONSTRUCTION, C. 1908. A new century brought feelings of progress and optimism. Accordingly, the freeholders commissioned J. Riley Gordon, Tracy and Swartout to design a new temple of justice. Construction began in 1907 with formal dedication of the edifice in 1909. Built at a cost of approximately $250,000, the impressive marble structure drew some critics at the time. An award-winning restoration of this magnificent landmark was completed in 1996.

DOME OF THE 1909 COURTHOUSE. Justice holds her scales aloft on the copper dome of the Beaux Arts style courthouse.

Five
Happenings and Disasters

ELEPHANTS ON MAIN STREET, 1907. Elephants on Main Street probably seemed as unusual then as they do today, but the message is clear: The Circus was in town! Somerville was on the main circus railway circuit during the golden age of the American circus. Barnum and Bailey's Circus was among those that pitched tents at West End.

CIRCUS PARADE DOWN WEST END ON CIRCUS DAY, JULY 2, 1907. These parades were held in the then-empty fields at the west end of town. The parade of colorful wagons and clowns passes by the Robert (on the left) and the Lindsley (on the right) mansions.

FERRIS WHEEL AT WEST END FIELD, 1907. The Ferris wheel was still a relative novelty when the circus brought this one to town. The wheel was one of the original attractions of the 1893 Chicago World's Fair. Today, carnivals and fairs seem incomplete without one.

SIDESHOWS, 1907. This particular year the circus ran for ten days—from July 3 to 13. It featured many of the era's popular sideshows for children, such as this Punch and Judy marionette show.

THE SOMERVILLE ATHLETIC CLUB, C. 1905. West End Field was the sight of numerous baseball games during an era when many towns had one or more local teams. The young men of Somerville's Athletic Club, with their distinctive shirts, include Reverend Pfantiehl, Wilbur Garretson, and Harold Halstead. Halstead was the first Somerville resident killed in action during World War I. (SMG.)

LINKS' CLAMBAKE AT CHIMNEY ROCK, C. 1927. Members and former members of the Lincoln Hose Company enjoyed annual fall outings at Chimney Rock. The crowd includes many well-known Somerville names including Tozzi, Schenck, Gernert, McAleavy, Stabile, Hall, and Hardgrove. Charles Staub posed with bottle in hand. Prohibition was not repealed until 1933. (FM.)

A GERMAINIA HALL THEATRICAL PRODUCTION, C. 1884. The cast of the *Barn Dance* took a final curtain call on Germainia Hall's Main Street stage. None of the players are identified, nor is the sponsoring organization. It is hoped there were at least as many persons in the audience as on the crowded stage.

STANDING ROOM ONLY AT THE HALL-MILLS TRIAL, 1926. The Hall-Mills case was the first sex scandal/murder of a century that unfortunately would see many such trials. The sensational trial brought legions of press and large, curious crowds to the courthouse. The defendants, the wife of the murdered minister and her three male relatives, were acquitted, making it one of America's greatest unsolved murders. (Special Collections, Rutgers University Libraries.)

JUSTICES CLEARY AND PARKER, 1926. Judge Frank L. Cleary (left) and State Court Justice Charles W. Parker listen intently to testimony in the Hall-Mills case. Unmoved by the trial's sensationalism, their faces betray little. Cleary, a Somerville resident, handled the preliminary hearing and stayed on at Parker's request for the grand jury and trial. Clarence E. Case, future justice of the State Supreme Court, was assistant defense counsel. (CCHC.)

A ROMANTIC COMEDY, C. 1900. Local dramatic productions were put on by members of church groups, the Monday Evening Club, or the West End Dramatic Society, which was affiliated with the fire department. The play and cast of characters shown here is unidentified, except for the white-haired man (second from the right), who is Clarence Case.

COMPANY H RIFLE TEAM, 1892. Company H Militiamen won the Inter-company Trophy for sharp shooting in September of 1892. From left to right are as follows: Corp. Irving Weaver, Sgt. John Wehrly, George Cramer, Capt. Gilbert Cook, Sgt. Charles Smith, and Corp. Edward Thompson. Several of these men fought in the Spanish-American War in 1898.

RECRUITING STATION, NO. 2, C. 1917. The Armory was where one got in line to fight the Kaiser. Company M was the National Guard unit based in Somerville. Members posed in front of the Armory, which served as the local recruiting station. Some wore shirt sleeves because uniforms were in short supply. The recruiters, seated in the front row, had done their job well.

COMPANY M, OCTOBER 1917. Before shipping out to Camp McClelland in Alabama, these young men posed on the steps of the new courthouse. They were the last of the 113th Infantry, which was composed of National Guard units. George Voorhees (center, first row) was the unit's captain. These men would fight in the Alsace, Argonne, and St. Mihiel campaigns. Of the two units mustered in Somerset Country, more than 400 men answered the call.

WASHINGTON'S BIRTHDAY, C. 1928. The Camp Frelinghuysen Chapter of the Daughters of the American Revolution gathered annually in the dining room of the Wallace House to celebrate General Washington's birthday. None of the ladies has been positively identified; however, the lone gentleman is Sen. Joseph Frelinghuysen, an active friend of the chapter for many years.

WELCOME HOME, SEPTEMBER 27, 1919. One of the largest parades Somerville has ever hosted was the Welcome Home Celebration given for the returning World War I veterans. Former Council President Louis Bellis was the grand marshall. In the lead car were Mayor Steele and Senator Frelinghuysen. Following were Lt. Herbert Davis, ranking officer of Company M; four members of the Army Nurse Corps from Somerset County; and finally the platoons of officers and enlisted men from the area. Lt. John W. Hardgrove Jr. led the first platoon. Thousands lined the route to view the 3,500 marchers, which included all Somerville and Branchburg schoolchildren, seven bands, and two fife and drum corps.

CROWING VICTORY, 1919. The end of World War I was greeted with an enthusiastic outpouring of patriotic feeling that was publicly demonstrated. The rooster, crowing victory, expressed these proud feelings. This view looks west on Main Street. The Regent Theater, dripping with American flags, is at the center. The West End (Ballantine) Building is visible on the far left. (BHS.)

INDIAN FLOAT, 1919. The Improved Order of Red Men, one of several fraternal organizations participating in the Welcome Home Parade, contributed a float depicting "Smoking the Peace Pipe." The white house in the background, later demolished, was the retirement home of confectioner Horatio Adams, who gave the world Black Jack Licorice and Chiclets gum.

Parade Lineup, 1919. Lining up at Cliff and Bridge Streets for the Welcome Home Parade is the float of the Knights of the Temple, another participating fraternal organization. The float following it was one of the most popular of the parade. Sponsored by Somerville Garage, it depicted the Kaiser as a caged "Beast of Berlin." Johnny Garrigan, who was inside the bear costume, told reporters that it was "his greatest stunt ever." However, he said that he was somewhat reluctant to repeat his effort because the costume was hot and a number of boys poked him with sticks rather unmercifully. The Adams' house is again visible in the background.

ELKS' CONVOCATION, C. 1909. The Regent Theater hosted an Elks' Convocation sometime prior to World War I. The group in front is Oberbrunner's Orchestra, which played for many local events. Mr. Oberbrunner himself is on piano. On the right is Paul Wildgen (trumpet) with Andrew and Ferd Hoch. On the left is John Purcell (violin), who served in World War I.

THE LADIES AUXILIARY, C. 1912. The proceeds from this bazaar booth or refreshment stand, perhaps at the Decoration Day or Veteran's Day parade, no doubt went to some worthy cause. The location is unknown, but the building may possibly be either old Somerset Hospital or the old Elks Club.

LINCOLN HOSE ON PARADE, C. 1897. Firemen often marched in parades to show solidarity with neighboring towns. The first members of the Lincoln Hose Co. are the leading group. Third from the right is John Wehrly, soon to earn the rank of captain during the Spanish-American War. Employed by the *Gazette* in civilian life, his reports from training camp on the experiences of Somerville boys kept the folks at home informed.

PUMPER, C. 1900. A crowd gathers to watch the fire department's steam pumper in action as a wood frame building in town burns. (FM.)

THE IRON WORKS FIRE, JULY 1909. Fires often drew crowds of the curious as they still do today. At a safe distance, a throng observes the efforts to douse a fire at the Somerville Iron Works. Note the boy in the tree. The blaze was well underway when the horse-drawn equipment arrived. Several firemen were injured, but no one was killed. Damages were about $100,000, a huge sum in those days.

FIRE AT UNIONIST GAZETTE, FEBRUARY 1917. The three-story brick Unionist Gazette plant was left a burnt-out shell. The fire, starting in the dead of night, was well underway before the alarm sounded. Linotypes and heaving machinery crashed from the second floor into the cellar of "Association Hall." Tenants living in apartments above the newspaper office nearly suffocated. They were carried down ladders to safety. (FM.)

FREIGHT HOUSE FIRE, SEPTEMBER 1912. Jersey Central Railroad's freight house, the Vroom Mill office, and Gallagher's icehouse were destroyed by a blaze that consumed the west side of South Bridge Street. Firemen were severely hampered by low water pressure. A catastrophe was averted when a freight car with dynamite was hauled out of the area by a quick-thinking railroad engineer. Here, the still steaming rubble is hosed down.

WINTER BLITZ. In 1888, New Jersey experienced one of the heaviest snowfalls on record. This picture records the aftermath of that blizzard on Main Street. Wagons piled high with snow head out of town for dumping. The vapor from the horses nostrils attests to their effort in the frigid air. The Ten Eyck Hotel on the corner of Division Street is in the background.

TROLLEY IN THE SNOW, 1905. This special vehicle had a snowplow attached. This photo may record the first mechanized plowing in town in the aftermath of a heavy snowfall, most likely around the turn of the century. Technology may have changed, but digging out after a big snowstorm is an experience we all know too well.

FLOODS, 1903. This apparently tranquil scene is misleading. It shows a flooded Bridge Street flowing past Dakin's carriage house, just north of Cliff Street. October of 1903 saw New Jersey's "Great Deluge and Flood." A storm dumped 15.5 inches of rain on the state, setting a longstanding record for the worst flooding in state history. It stood unbroken until 1955.

Six
In Case of Emergency

HORSELESS AMBULANCE, C. 1920. The hospital superintendent and head nurse, Miss Josephine Hamilton, and her nursing staff pose with the hospital's new motorized ambulance. This ambulance could be summoned dialing 119, a reversal of the standard 911 emergency number by sheer coincidence.

SOMERSET HOSPITAL, C. 1901. In 1898, a 16-year-old boy died from a head injury due to lack of prompt medical attention. Local citizens and physicians organized and began raising funds to purchase an East Main Street home, formerly the Lord property. After the installation of electricity and running water, Somerset Hospital opened its doors in 1900. There were 10 physicians on staff and 13 beds. (SMG.)

STAFF PHYSICIANS, C. 1916. Eight members of the medical staff pose outside the expanded hospital. From left to right are Drs. Runkle F. Hegeman, A. Anderson Lawton, Claudius Fisher, Aaron L. Stillwell, Thomas Flynn, B.F. Seaman, William H. Long, and Charles F. Halstead. Dr. Long also served as the school physician. In 1998, the old "house-hospital" still stands near the intersection of East Main and Rehill. (SCHS.)

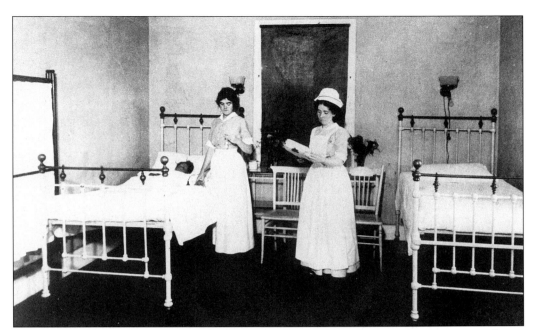

NURSES ON THE WARD, C. 1913. The hospital at first had just three employees; two are shown here. Although medical technology has advanced, the standard routine of checking pulse and recording vital signs on the patients' charts has remained unchanged. In its first year, 46 patients were admitted. A nursing school was founded in 1911 in order to provide trained, competent care in the growing hospital. (SAC.)

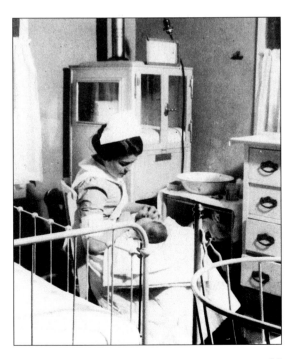

NEWBORN NURSERY, C. 1920. The small house was expanded several times during the period between 1911 and 1925 to accommodate the increased demand for services. The hospital offered a new maternity ward and postpartum care. Each baby was given a necklace with his or her name to prevent mix-ups and which families could purchase as a keepsake. This was the method accepted "at the very best institutions," wrote Nursing Superintendent Hamilton. (SAC.)

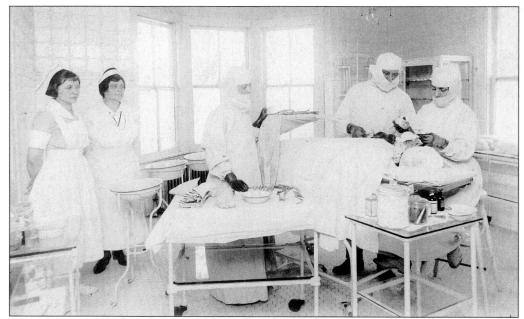

O.R., C. 1920. The tiled operating room (the former front parlor) was state of the art in its day. It was equipped with high-powered electric illumination so that surgery could be performed even at night. It was reportedly the best equipped facility outside of New York City.

HOSPITAL NURSING STAFF, 1925. A fund-raising campaign was inaugurated to build a new, 100-bed, brick facility. Student nurses (front), full-fledged RNs (back row), and a full-time hospital dietician, Ms. Ann Wolf (second row, far right) join Superintendent Katherine MacCollum (second row, third from the right) on the steps of the new hospital. Constructed by the firm of Crow, Lewis and Wick, the new hospital was located on Rehill Avenue. (SAC.)

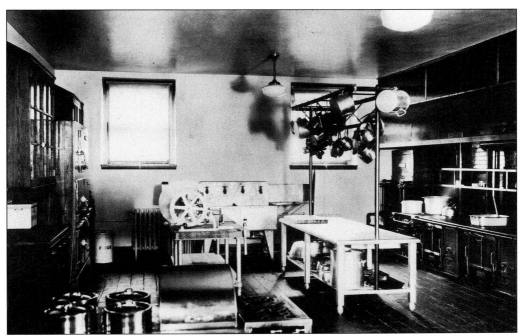

HOSPITAL KITCHEN, C. 1925. The hospital's new state-of-the-art, full-service kitchen was the domain of Ann Wolf and her staff. It featured a coal stove and several iceboxes. (SAC.)

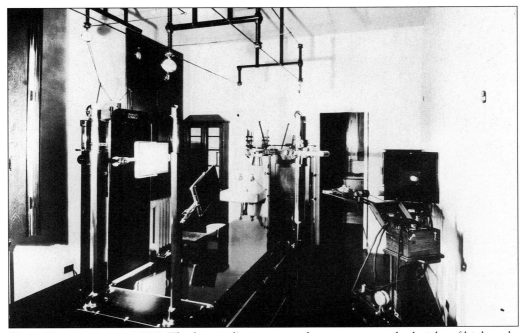

X-RAY DEPARTMENT, 1925. The hospital's new x-ray department was the height of high tech. Discovered just 30 years before in Germany, the new technology rapidly became an indispensable diagnostic tool of twentieth-century medicine. (SAC.)

Satisfied Patient, 1925. A young patient relaxes in the solarium of the new pediatric ward, concluding a four-week "visit" as it was called. He had sustained a compound fracture of his forearm. The cast was discreetly covered for the photograph. The cost for his care—nothing; he was considered a charity patient. (SAC.)

Red Cross Poster, c. 1917. The list of organizers of Somerville's American Red Cross chapter reads like a "Who's Who" of early-twentieth-century Somerville. Established in 1917, the kickoff rally was held in the Armory with a capacity crowd. This vintage poster was used to solicit local donations. After the war, a home visiting nurse program and first-aid classes were established.

LEVERICH HOSE CARRIAGE, C. 1874. This hose carriage recalls the early days of Somerville's volunteer fire department. The town has long been concerned with the safety of its residents. The first fire company was organized in 1835, the police force in 1889, the first hospital 1899, and the rescue squad (New Jersey's first inland squad) in 1928. (FM.)

DECORATION DAY, C. 1900. Engine Company, No. 1, Somerville's oldest company, reorganized from earlier companies in 1878 when the board of commissioners purchased the first steam-powered engine. George Totten (second row, second from right), son of the first company foreman, rang the town's first fire bell in 1911. This bell is displayed on Borough Hall's lawn.

INSPECTION DAY, OCTOBER 1912. Inspection Day is an October tradition in the fire department. Here the men of Lincoln Chemical Engine Co. 4 turn out in front of the firehouse. As they do today, men from all walks of life volunteered to protect their community. Identified in this photo are Larry O'Donnell Sr. (front left), William H. Cawley Jr. (middle), Larry Austin (behind to Cawley's right), and Tom Van Ness (left of fence). (FM.)

ARCHIE BRUNT, C. 1888. The pride of the Somerville Volunteers is apparent from this photo of an early member of the Lincoln Hose Company. He posed not only in his uniform, but with his fire helmet as well. (SCHS.)

OUR LAST TRIP, OCTOBER 31, 1912. Larry O' Donnell Sr. leads Grace and her partner, Maude, out for a final parade on Inspection Day. The team of white mares had served Lincoln Chemical and the town faithfully from 1898 to 1912; they retired to a Neshanic farm. Assisting driver Hugh McAleavy is Charles Gernert. Both were Main Street merchants. (FM.)

FIRST DAY ON THE JOB, 1912. Replacing horses Grace and Maude were Duke and Baron, driven in this photo by Larry Austin. The horses served a little more than ten years, retiring in 1923. They were replaced by motorized equipment. Austin also drove the first motor truck until his own retirement. (FM.)

SEAGRAVE ENGINE ON PARADE, C. 1918. The Hook and Ladder Company's horse-drawn engine was acquired by the board of commissioners in 1909 for $2,000 and remained in service until 1923. The driver is David Hardgrove with his son, James (known as "Bud"), sitting next to him, ready to wave at the crowds in one of the town's parades. The World War I veterans include Otto Lechtietner (far right).

HOSE-KEEPING CHORES, C. 1922. By the twenties, the town's firefighting equipment was becoming increasingly motorized. The first horseless vehicle, purchased in 1916, was a Mack chemical and hose truck. Superintendent of Maintenance Cramer Fisher, assisted by John Purcell, tend to the business of hose maintenance on the new hose truck. (FM.)

Seven
Commerce and Industry

A BUSINESS FOR THE AGES, C. 1870. John Wagoner owned this elegant Victorian hearse, pictured at the intersection of Doughty Avenue and Main Street. Maxwell King is the driver. Wagoner operated a bridle and saddle business in town since at least 1829. The original St. John's Episcopal Church (1851–1895) stands in the background. The shed to the right belonged to the Union Engine Co., an early Somerville fire company. (SCHS.)

STEVENS HARNESS SHOP, C. 1910. The harness shop owned by the Stevens family was located at 167 West Main Street in the building that was once the Baptist Meeting House. Stevens's granddaughter, now age 90, remembers visiting there. The signs show that the owner was diversifying his inventory as the days of the horse and buggy drew to a close—the store also carried awnings and auto trim!

ROSS BRICKYARD, C. 1900. Located on 16 acres north of Spring Street in the area of Walck Park, the Ross Brickyard was a significant Somerville business venture. Bricks were actually made at the site. After firing, they were stacked and stored in the large sheds shown in the background.

OLD RAILROAD DEPOT, 1890. Somerville did not always have its beautiful train station. This simple wooden structure served as a temporary depot after the original station was destroyed by fire in 1867. The exact date of the first construction is unknown, but most likely dates from the railroad's first reaching Somerville in the 1840s. The railroad was a key player in Somerville's development over almost a 100-year period.

GUNZELMAN AND CRAMER LUMBERYARD, C. 1901. Construction workers pose for a picture during the building of the Gunzelman and Cramer Lumberyard Office. The lumberyard was located at the site of the Downtown Municipal Parking Lot.

SOMERVILLE IRON WORKS, C. 1913. Located on Fairview Avenue between James and Haynes Streets, this major industrial plant produced pipes and gas stoves from 1905 to 1945. With offices in several U.S. cities, the plant was managed by William Kirby. Attracted by steady pay, teenage boys often dropped out of school to work there. The little girl, possibly Kirby's daughter, adds a soft touch to the photo.

A BUSINESS TRANSACTION, C. 1900. Two unidentified businessmen discuss matters in a gas-lit office—most likely a realty or insurance firm, such as Nolan and Swinton. Located at 12 West Main Street, the firm wrote fire, life, accident, plate glass, liability, and burglary insurance, and "took an active interest in real estate business," according to a contemporary account. (SCHS.)

BROCKWAY CARRIAGE AGENCY, C. 1898. Although the railroad brought commerce and travelers to town, some Somerville businesses continued to serve the need for the traditional modes of transportation. Willard Durham, his son, and Jake Henry (from left to right) stand in front of this Main Street shop, which sold carriages and harnesses to accommodate those who traveled by the four-legged mode of transportation.

LIVERY STABLE, C. 1895. Serving several different community needs, Newton Dunster not only leased and boarded horses, but also moved and stored furniture "with care" at his location on 15 Division Street. The stable burnt down about 1913. Ironically, Dunster was a member of the Engine Co., No. 1 and drove the horse-drawn Amoskeag steamer. The scene is reminiscent of the Old West rather than New Jersey. (SCHS.)

WOOLEN MILL, C. 1913. The site of a late-twentieth-century apartment complex and storefronts, this Main Street building once housed the DeWitte Dyeing and Bleaching Works. Specializing in woolen, worsted, and cotton yarns, the business provides another example of Somerville's varied commercial and industrial past.

DIX SEWING CO., 1920. Located on Doughty Avenue, this ladies dress and uniform factory was representative of many garment factories operating throughout New Jersey before World War II. The trolley provided a convenient means of transportation to the building from surrounding areas.

AUTOMOBILE AND BICYCLE SHOP, C. 1895. Garretson's shop on Main Street was an omen of things to come. Probably the first automobile dealer in town, Garretson also sold bicycles, an extremely popular item in the late 1880s. Automobile dealers have come and gone, but bicycles have remained important to Somerville, home of the race known as "the Tour of Somerville" and the U.S. Bicycling Hall of Fame.

NORTON GREENHOUSES, C. 1910. These greenhouses once fronted on Somerset Street but were demolished in the mid-1980s. Plants were grown and sold on both a retail and wholesale basis. Owner Anson Norton was fire chief around 1913.

ENGINE 999 AT SOMERVILLE STATION, C. 1925. Many Somerville businesses were located on or near the railroad track. Engines like this transported passengers and freight. The railbeds were raised and upgraded in 1912. The mid-twenties was again a time of modernization by Central Railroad of New Jersey with major improvements undertaken in Somerville.

VROOM MILL, C. 1925. This South Bridge Street structure located near the railroad track was a working coal and feed mill in the early half of the century. Feed was ground, loaded, and stored on the premises. Former mayor Robert Adams managed the facility. In recent years, the building was owned by Ted Sargent, who donated the structure to the borough.

HAMILTON STREET, 1925. This view, looking up Hamilton toward Main Street, shows some of the improvements made all along the railroad. The steam shovel was used to excavate land for a new abutment. The horse-drawn wagon contrasts with the heavy industrial machinery of the modern age.

SOMERSET STREET, C. 1924. The steel panels of the Somerset Street train overpass were set in place by crane on December 16. The panel shown is 75 feet long and weighs about 44 tons. The spectators and automobiles provide some perspective.

CRON'S DRUG STORE, C. 1920. An attractive awning announces the location of Cron's Drug Store to passersby in downtown Somerville. Businessmen mull over the day's events as commerce takes its daily course in the busy borough. (FM.)

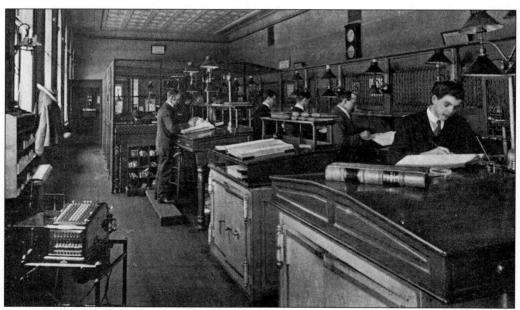

TELLERS AT FIRST NATIONAL, 1908. Tellers and bookkeepers labor intently behind the grilled counters at the Maple and Main Street bank. Note the early adding machine on the small cart in the left foreground. The large ledgers on the desk were either account or signature books. In contrast to later methods of security, bound books held sample signatures for verification of each depositor's check endorsements.

Eight
Just Plain Folks

SOMERVILLE ELEMENTARY, JUNE 25, 1914. Gus Wissert, who saved this picture of his grade-school chums of nearly 80 years ago, is in the top row and second from right. He is about seven years old in the picture.

THE KLINE CHILDREN, C. 1860. Philadelphia artist Jonathan K. Trego painted Jacob Kline Jr. (center) and his siblings. Son of a local gristmill operator, Kline spent most of his life in Somerville. His business ventures included the grocery of Hardgrove and Kline and later the Vroom Mill. He died in 1911. His only surviving daughter, the last of the family, donated this portrait to the library.

LUCY SCHENK, C. 1870. Born in 1802, this African-American freewoman and her husband lived and raised a family locally. Many of their descendants still reside in Somerville. In 1872, she and Henry celebrated their golden wedding anniversary, an event written up in the *Unionist Gazette*. New Jersey passed a gradual emancipation law in 1804.

Riding with the Grocer, c. 1890. A young Miss Brokaw enjoys a ride in H.A. Green's delivery wagon. Green was one of Somerville's many grocers. The Star Grocery, his store at 30 West Main, sold "nothing but First Class Goods." Orders were arranged at doorside when the wagon called at 7 a.m., with home delivery later that day. Many types of perishable commodities were delivered by wagon.

Central Cash Grocers, September 1910. Those wishing to select their own fresh produce could patronize Bachmann and Van Tine grocery, which specialized in fresh produce. Wearing cap, tie, and apron, young Van Tine stands ready to assist his customers. He was killed in World War I.

INDIAN PRINCESS, C. 1913. The Antituberculosis Society sponsored an Independence Day pageant that presented highlights from American history. Held on the Duke Estate, it was organized by Miss Maude Davenport, a local dance instructor. Her students dramatized the rescue of Capt. John Smith by Pocahontas. This unidentified young lady either participated in the program, or was inspired to imitate an older sister.

SKATING AT ROSS BRICKYARD, C. 1929. Ross Brickyard's property featured a small pond, located north of Spring Street. When it froze solid, children gathered there to skate on bright, crisp winter days.

JUNIOR FIRE DEPARTMENT. Boys doing things boys enjoy were photographed around 1905 in a typical Somerville backyard. The game involved playing fire department. The helmet, looking suspiciously large, was probably "borrowed" from a dad.

THREE CYCLISTS, C. 1900. Right in style with the latest model bicycles, these young Somerville gentlemen pose for the camera. From left to right, they are Loney Stevens, Larry O'Donnell, and Henry Stevenson. The modern bicycle frame replaced the older velocipede, with its large front wheel, about 1899. Bicycling was advocated in the late 1890s for health and fitness, much as running and aerobics are today.

GIRLS' BASKETBALL, C. 1901. Girls' basketball may have been the first team sport offered to young ladies at the public high school. Two of the Vanderveer girls made the team. In front with the jaunty white-tied middy is Kay. A niece of Dr. Mary Gaston, she would become the county's first welfare director. Directly behind her is Elizabeth Dodd Vanderveer. The team played outdoors because the school had no gymnasium.

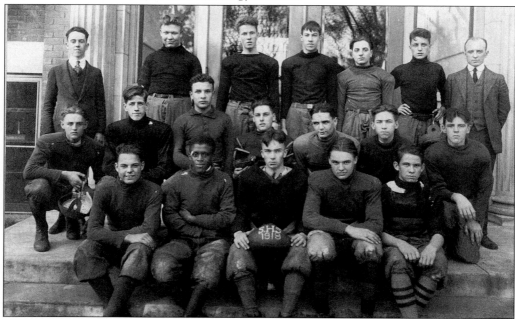

PIONEER FOOTBALL TEAM, 1919. The soon-to-be county champions posed in in front of Elementary School No. 2. Principal Billy Holbert (far right) and athletic instructor Jim Nash (standing left) were the coaches. Pants were issued by the school, but the boys supplied their own jerseys. Helmets were leather and no padding was worn. Prominent local names on the team were Hoffman, Stires, Granetz, and Kline. (SMG.)

WINNING STREAK. The 1918–1919 basketball squad was the first team fielded after the five-year hiatus caused by World War I. Starting late and without a coach, the team's winning 10-2 season was all the more remarkable. In the back row, the players, from left to right, are Eugene Stack, Byron Davenport, and George Hoffman. Standing is manager Joe Hickey. Seated from left to right are John Beekman, George Bird, Sam Woldin (captain), Harry Nixon, and John Hlafter. (BOE.)

CLASS OF 1908. The very proper Class of 1908 numbered just 20 students. Among them were several members of the Shapiro family and (first row) Mr. Irving Schwed (second from left) and Mr. Charles Wehrly (fifth from left); (second row) Miss Helen Staats (left), Miss Eleanor Brokaw (third from left), and Miss Albertine Wehrly (fourth from left); (last row, center) Miss Helen Case.

PRIMARY ROOM, SCHOOL NO. 3, C. 1910. Posing outside the wooden-frame "Colored School" on Cliff and Davenport Streets is a class of 49 children with their teacher (back right), probably Mrs. Rumson, the A.M.E. minister's wife. Young Mr. Doman (fifth child from right) later became a school custodian. A school for African-American children, founded by local African-American women, existed as early as 1857. It became part of the public school system in 1868.

CENTRAL SCHOOL, C. 1920. In this class, possibly sixth grade, William Sutphen and George Shay appear in the front row (fifth and sixth from left). Shay would later teach history and civics at Somerville High in the 1930s and would become one of Somerville's most popular mayors. Sutphen served the county as a justice of the peace. Other well-known local names represented are Pessaroff, Ten Eyck, Totten, Richards, and Van Fleet.

CLASS OF 1925. R. Anna Miller (on the far right) is pictured with Somerville's scholars in front of the second high school (middle school in 1998). She wrote a lively account of her tenure, which extended from the mid-1890s until her retirement in the 1930s. High school was a two-year course when Miller began to teach, and few students completed even this course.

CLASS OF 1920. Shown on the front porch of Somerville's first public school are the 33 members of the Class of 1920. George Hoffman (top row, left) would later become the borough's first African-American councilman. (BOE.)

CLASS PLAY, 1926. The cast of the senior play *Nothing but the Truth* is shown with Miss Feinman, their English teacher and drama coach (back row, far left). The title of their production echoes the courtroom oath—the choice of production was perhaps inspired by the infamous Hall-Mills trial underway at the courthouse.

A TOUCH OF CLASS, C. 1926. In the 1920s, Somerville High's senior class made an annual pilgrimage to Mount Vernon. This commemorative of the Class of 1926 is particularly precious, for it was autographed by 41 students. Among them were family names still prominent in the

ORIENT BUCKBOARD, 1904. George Andros and Helen H. Thomson take their first car out for a spin on a fine summer's day. This may have been one of the earliest motorized vehicles in town. Note the still unpaved street. Many New Jersey roads were not paved until after World War I.

town and the county, like Louis Marsjanik, Grace Studdiford, George Shay (later mayor), Jack M. Torpey, and Charles Palmer.

MEN ABOUT TOWN, C. 1916. Near the Central Garage on Warren and Main, a number of dapper gentlemen pose with a late model roadster. Standing to the left is Edward L. Ramsey, a veteran of both World Wars; he retired from the service with the rank of colonel.

MAIN STREET GROUP, C. 1900. This group, including Mr. Wachter (left), and Larry O'Donnell Sr. (second from left), posed outside a Main Street shop. Young Alfred Hoch in knickers with his bicycle is standing with his father, Ferd (in derby), and Raymond O'Donell Sr. (bowtie). Other turn-of-the-century indicators are the summer straw hats which retailed on Main Street for between 25¢ and $2.40 according to Thomas & Co.'s ad from the period.

U.S. Post Office, c. 1900. The Somerville post office was located in the Gaston Building on Main Street until 1923 when it relocated to 30 Division Street. The men pictured here were Somerville's first letter carriers to deliver door to door. They are, from left to right, as follows: George Drobny, J.C. Garretson, James Jones, and Harry Dietz. (USPO.)

Clambake, 1925. During the twenties, the men of Lincoln Hose Co. enjoyed an annual social gathering at Chimney Rock. Tony Tozzi, in coveralls, was the chairman of this annual fireman's event. The banner, used yearly, read, "I am the Commander." The others pictured are, from left to right, as follows: (seated) Howard Perry and Mr. Allgair; (standing) Charles Fetesly, Charles Matthews Sr., and Ed Wittenbech. (FM.)

POOLE-CASE WEDDING, OCTOBER 1906. The wedding party of Albert E. Case and Mary B. Poole was photographed at the Poole home on West High. Among the various members are future State Supreme Court Justice Clarence E. Case (standing, fifth from left) and Clifford P. Case, future U.S. senator (standing, far right).

Nine
Home Sweet Home

DORMITORY ROOM, C. 1911. When Somerset Hospital opened its own training school for nurses in 1911, dormitory rooms were provided so that student nurses could live and work in proximity to the East Main Street hospital. Students' rooms were quite comfortable and homey, giving these young women a sense of independence and professional pride.

JOSHUA DOUGHTY'S HOUSE, C. 1857. This Victorian version of the Parsonage appears on an 1857 Somerville map. It was then home to Joshua Doughty and stood at the foot of the street that bears his name. The side wing was not original and was demolished when the house was moved to Washington Place. The Dutch Parsonage served as a temporary site of the Queens College prep school during the American Revolution.

THE MIDDAUGH-MANN HOUSE, 1929. Vying for the title of "oldest house in town," this Washington Place house may incorporate the fieldstone foundation and walls of an older colonial homestead. Middaugh was the son-in-law of original settler Peter Van Neste. The house was rebuilt after a fire damaged the earlier farmhouse, and it was enlarged several times between 1800 and 1820. The Richards family owned the home from 1926 until 1968.

LINDSLEY HOUSE, WEST END. This sketch of a classic Italianate home shows a house that can still be seen on West End near Borough Hall. Originally owned by the Lindsley family from its construction until 1933, it eventually became a funeral home. The building's original style has not been changed in all that time. The source of this photo, an illustrated 1857 map, gives much information about the character of Somerville in the mid-1800s.

THE EMERY HOUSE. South Street all but disappeared along with this Second Empire home in the cause of urban renewal in 1970. Now a parking garage, it was once the home of the Emery family. John Rockafeller Emery was a financial agent for Central Railroad of New Jersey and the Lehigh-Wilkes Barre Coal Company. A deacon and elder of the Second Reformed Church, he helped lay out Somerville's New Cemetery.

MESSLER HOUSE. Now the site of a shopping mall, 78–84 West Main was once the home of Rev. Abraham Messler, pastor of the First Reformed Church from 1832 to 1882. Built sometime after 1812, this house was demolished about 1919. It was one of the last private homes of the Federal period along Main Street.

SAMUEL MILLER HOUSE, 1857. Samuel Miller built this Greek Revival house on property once part of the Wallace Farm. It was later the Reverend Frederick Cornell's home. Kate Claxon (nee Cole), a famous actress of the Victorian stage, was born in the back parlor. The house was purchased in 1928 by Chief Justice Clarence E. Case and remained in his family until 1997.

S.S. Hartwell House. S.S. Hartwell, a major Somerville property holder, built this grand Greek Revival home on the southwest corner of Main and Bridge Streets. The Lincoln-style top hat of the well-dressed man on the veranda suggests the mid-1860s. The photograph is nearly identical to the 1857 map sketch, confirming this date.

THE "CORNER HOUSE." The fine Victorian house that stood on the corner of Bridge and West High Street was the home of the Gaston family. It was constructed in 1859 by Hugh M. Gaston, the prominent local attorney who drafted Somerville's 1862 charter. Dr. Mary Gaston, his daughter, later lived and held office hours there. The house, one of four grand homes on the block, was badly damaged by fire in 1973 and subsequently demolished.

ANOTHER GASTON HOME. This home on West High Street was the residence of Louis P. Gaston, son of Hugh and brother of Dr. Mary. Constructed approximately the same time as the Corner House, this house was demolished in 1961 to make way for an office building.

DR. WILLIAM LONG AND NEIGHBOR, C. 1910. Dr. Long was the school physician, and Mrs. Long, a descendant of the Tunison family, was renowned for her beautiful garden. In 1857, both of these houses were owned by the Tunisons. A neighboring home, not shown but still standing, was the parsonage of the Methodist church.

ANDREW CROSS HOME. This West End home shown on the 1857 map has long since been replaced with modern construction. However, it was a very popular style with local builders. Until the late 1800s, carpenters often built homes from sample "pattern books" and tended to specialize in one or two basic styles. Several homes in town share nearly identical features to this one.

HOPE-CASE HOUSE, C. 1871. Constructed in 1851 in the popular castellated style for the First National Bank's president A.D. Hope, this High Street home has sported several architectural styles. Here, it is shown remodeled in the Italianate style by the Ballantine family. Justice Clarence E. Case, who restored it early in this century to a Greek Revival appearance, had his law library there. The wooden street sign on the fence reads, "High Street."

Dr. Simmes Craig Home, c. 1865. A square box style with hipped roof, Dr. Craig's home preceded the Somerset Trust building on the corner of Main and Maple. The building next door appears to be a grocery, but the 1857 map lists it as a barber shop.

Mountain Avenue, Near Main, c. 1898. This home still stands but without its Victorian porch, which was a late addition. Originally built as a typical New Jersey I–plan farmhouse with a fieldstone foundation, it was probably constructed after the Civil War on property belonging to John Whitenack.

J.B. LOSEY'S HOME, 1913. In addition to its Victorian houses, Somerville also boasts vintage early-twentieth-century dwellings. This "workingman's four-square" was typical of the styles of this period. The Loseys were partners of latter-day Tunisons in a wholesale grocery and pork packery near the old train depot. Fresh country pork sausage was a specialty.

THE NURSES RESIDENCE, C. 1920. Another early-twentieth-century house design is illustrated by this bungalow. It was located on Grant Avenue and was donated to the hospital for use as a nurses' residence in 1913 by J. Harper Smith's widow, Mary. A very comfortable and attractive style, many similar well-crafted bungalows were built in Somerville.

ON THE FRONT PORCH, C. 1900. This is a modest family home, probably on Cliff Street, where many houses of similar style and vintage still exist. The exact location is difficult to pinpoint since many houses have lost their distinctive carpentry or been altered over the years.

CORNER CLIFF AND ROSS STREETS, C. 1906. This view of the corner home and its neighbors up the street shows a typical middle-class neighborhood in early-twentieth-century Somerville. Ranging in style, several of these homes still stand today, although the old-fashioned mailbox and hitching posts are gone. The corner house is gone too, but a very similar one still occupies another Somerville corner.

HOMETOWN VIEW, C. 1910. This view of residential Somerville was taken from the roof of the old county jail on Grove Street. The view looks northeast toward the Watchung Hills and the still largely undeveloped eastern portion of town.